TULSA CITY-COUNTY LIBRARY

THE ESSENTIAL GUIDE

Disney

PLANES

THE ESSENTIAL GUIDE

Written by Steve Bynghall

CONTENTS

INTRODUCTION

In the rural town of Propwash Junction, Dusty Crophopper spends his days spraying the surrounding fields with fertilizer. But the agricultural plane does not want to be crop-dusting all his life. He has big and bold dreams of becoming a professional racing plane and seeing the world by competing in the annual Wings Around The Globe Rally, the ultimate around-the-world race challenge!

Although some say his head is in the clouds, Dusty is determined to succeed and practices every day with the help of Propwash Junction pal Chug. However, Dusty soon realizes he has a sky-high set of hurdles to climb. Not only is his racing technique poor and his engine stretched to its limits, but he is also terrified of heights!

When Dusty enlists the help of war veteran Skipper as his mentor, his new career may just have a chance of taking off ...

Fasten your seat belts!

DUSTY

Dusty Crophopper is no ordinary crop duster—this agricultural plane has big ambitions to race in the famous Wings Around The Globe Rally! But with a fear of heights and an engine not made for racing, it is not easy. Only Dusty's determination can make his dream come true!

Dusty's nose is capped, which makes it stronger

NKRH911

" LOOK, I AM MORE THAN JUST A CROP DUSTER!"

DOWN ON THE FARM

Every day, hardworking Dusty sprays smelly fertilizer on the fields around Propwash Junction to help make the crops grow. It's a dirty job, but someone has to do it!

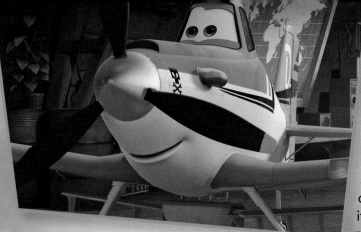

Vertical stabilizer and rudder on tail

BIG DREAMS

Dusty has loved racing since he was young. He has followed heroes like Ripslinger for years, and always daydreams about his own racing career taking off. Now it is time to put the plans into action!

TRUE OR FALSE?

When Dusty first races he calls himself Turbo Tailspin.

FALSE! He calls himself Strut Jetstream.

When Dusty flies to JFK International Airport in New York for the start of the WATG Rally, he is amazed by the Big Apple. Dusty has never been anywhere so big, busy, and bright before!

Wings designed for flying low

Tools of the trade—an M-5000 model sprayer

DOWN-TO-EARTH DUSTY

Dusty is a popular plane with lots of pals. He knows he needs the support of his friends to succeed. Even when he is the center of attention, Dusty's wheels stay firmly on the runway. However, he loves the name his friend Chug creates for him—Strut Jetstream!

DUSTY'S TOP 3:
EXERCISES IN THE AIR

★ Get a teacher for training

★ Think like a racer!

★ Stay focussed and overcome your fears

Welcome to Propwash Junction

Located in the middle of Minnesota, USA, quiet Propwash Junction is more of a place to pass through than visit. There is not really much to see in this sleepy little town, but the friendly townsfolk will always give you a warm welcome!

LIFE ON A HIGH PLAIN

Propwash Junction is surrounded by spectacular mountains and beautiful countryside. The town itself is perched on a plain sitting high on the cliff tops. Beautiful cornfields surround the town.

DUSTY'S HANGOUT

Dusty's hangar is full of his favorite things, including a map of the Wings Around The Globe air rally route and pictures of past champions!

CHUG AND DOTTIE'S FILL 'N' FLY

The service station is the social center of Propwash Junction. The locals drop by to have a chat with Chug and Dottie, as well as to get a fuel fill-up or a repair and tune-up. Dottie keeps spare parts for plane repairs inside.

ALL UNDER CONTROL

Air traffic control ensures everything runs smoothly at the town airport—not that there is much traffic in this pretty rural town!

SKIPPER'S HANGOUT

Skipper's hangar proudly flies the insignia of the Jolly Wrenches, his old navy squadron. This fighter plane spends a lot of time alone with his memories here.

CHUG

Friendly fuel truck Chug is happy serving customers at Propwash Junction's Fill 'n' Fly service station. When not working he supports best pal Dusty's racing dreams by helping him practice. Chug might not have such big plans himself, but this popular resident of Propwash Junction is always upbeat and will never let you down!

TRUE OR FALSE?

Chug opens a stall selling "official" Dusty merchandise.

TRUE! It even sells spinning mugs!

Roof keeps the sun out of Chug's eyes

Chrome emblem is always kept clean and shiny

BEST BUDDIES

Chug loves to relax in the hangar with best buddy Dusty, sipping a can of oil and watching the Racing Sports Network. These guys are perfect pals and can talk about racing all day long!

AT YOUR SERVICE

If you need fuel to go, Chug is your guy! He takes great pride in his work, and finds filling up most fulfilling. This creative fuel truck also makes and sells "official" Dusty souvenirs.

TRAVELING TRUCK

Chug is a homebody and has no great wish to see the world. However, he is very excited when he gets to travel to Mexico to see his best buddy Dusty race.

"FUELED AND READY, MAN!"

Occasionally Chug struggles to get his words out straight. Luckily he always has his good friends at Propwash Junction to help him get it right!

Fuel tank and nozzle for filling up planes

CHUG'S TOP 3: NICKNAMES FOR DUSTY

★ Duster

★ Dustmeister

★ Dusterino

13

A DAY IN THE LIFE OF A *Crop Duster*

Crop-dusting is not the most glamorous or exciting job, but Dusty takes pride in his work. Unfortunately, it does mean spraying muck over the same cornrows every day and reeking of the smelly fertilizer Vita-minamulch! For a dreamer like Dusty, the day passes by very slowly.

BOSSY PLANE

Dusty starts his day with a briefing from his boss, Leadbottom. This bad-tempered biplane loves crop-dusting, and has no time to entertain Dusty's dreams of becoming a racing plane.

OVER THE FIELDS

Dusty has to fly low and slow over the fields to make sure all crops get a good covering of fertilizer. It is repetitive work, but as he sprays, he can daydream about what it would be like to be a racer.

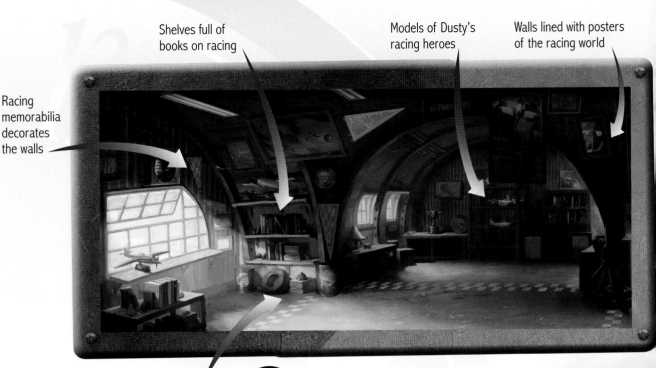

Shelves full of
books on racing

Models of Dusty's
racing heroes

Walls lined with posters
of the racing world

Racing
memorabilia
decorates
the walls

Plenty of space
for Dusty and his
pals to hang out

HOME SWEET HOME

Dusty's pad is the perfect place to unwind
after a hard day's crop-dusting. His TV is always
turned on to the Racing Sports Network, so that
he can keep up to date on all the latest air-racing news.

RALLY ROUTE

Dusty keeps a huge map
of the route of the Wings
Around The Globe Rally in his
hangar. Every evening he studies
the map and wonders what it
would be like to travel the world.

DID YOU KNOW?

Dusty's boss loves
the tangy smell of Vita-
minamulch. It reminds
him of daffodils and
Sunday dinner!

DOTTIE

Dottie is the main mechanic at the Fill 'n' Fly service station. If you are ever in a fix, this straight talking tug will soon have you on the mend— her technical know-how and attention to detail is amazing! However, her best quality is that she cares about making everything better!

TRUE OR FALSE?

Dottie believes that Dusty has the perfect engine for racing.

FALSE! She is worried that it is not suitable for high speeds.

PERFECT PARTNERS

Dottie and Chug own the Fill 'n' Fly service station and are firm friends. Level-headed Dottie keeps her eye on the garage—and on Chug—to ensure everything runs smoothly.

"DON'T DO ANYTHING CRAZY! FLY SAFE!"

Always carry the right tools for the job!

Handy side-belt for tools

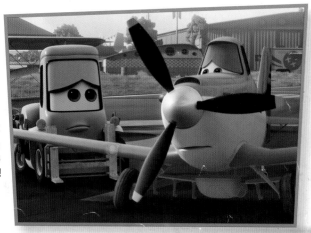

Despite her concerns about Dusty's high-flying dreams, Dottie still joins him at the Wings Around The Globe qualifiers— just in case she is needed to fix him. Being a skilled mechanic, Dottie is perfect as Dusty's one-tug technical team!

PLAIN-SPEAKING TUG

Dottie is never afraid to speak her mind, especially when she is worried about her friends. She advises Dusty to give up racing, as she knows his engine is not built for it and could easily get damaged.

DOTTIE'S TOP 3:
WARNINGS TO DUSTY

★ You've worn out the engine seal!

★ It'll end in turbine failure!

★ You'll crash ... KABOOM!

A TRUE FRIEND

When Dottie realizes that Dusty is deadly serious about racing, she backs him all the way. Her common sense and skills as a mechanic help to make him a success.

Forklifts to carry tools and move equipment

SKIPPER

In his heyday, legendary war veteran Skipper was an inspirational flight instructor in the navy who trained troops and prepared planes for war. But these days the bad-tempered Corsair plane no longer flies. However, he signs up for one last battle, when he reluctantly agrees to train Dusty for the race of his life!

This old propeller still functions well!

TALL TALES

Skipper loves to tell his old war stories and tales of raids. Some say he even shot down as many as 50 enemy planes! However, the grouchy veteran is not entirely truthful about his memories ...

SKIPPER'S TOP 3:
RACING TIPS

★ Gravity is your ally, let it work for you

★ Avoid going too wide on turns

★ Fly high to catch tailwinds for extra speed

TRUE OR FALSE?

Skipper is an old Corsair type fighter aircraft.

TRUE! He also has a fine radial engine.

HANGAR HIDEOUT

Secretive Skipper is a loner and he spends a lot of time alone in his hangar, reflecting on his past. When he does leave the hangar, he relies on his friend Sparky to move him around.

"IT AIN'T HOW FAST YOU FLY, IT'S HOW YOU FLY FAST!"

Distinctive military blue paintwork

"JW" is short for the Jolly Wrenches

Skipper is a fantastic flight instructor and turns Dusty into a real racer. During the Wings Around The Globe Rally, Skipper still gives Dusty tips and tactics over the radio. They even develop an unlikely friendship!

BADGE OF HONOR

Skipper was once part of the Jolly Wrenches squadron, the toughest navy outfit around. He still proudly wears the piston-and-crosswrenches insignia.

Skipper's Tips and Tricks

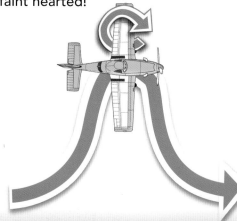

Skipper 1971

With so many years of flying experience, Skipper really knows his stuff. As Dusty's instructor, he is able to guide him through all the key tricks and maneuvers and correct him on his sloppy rolls and too-wide turns. Come on, we have a lot of work to do here!

Roll

With speed, take a 180 degree turn of the body so that you end upside-down. Stay cool and hang on to your hat!

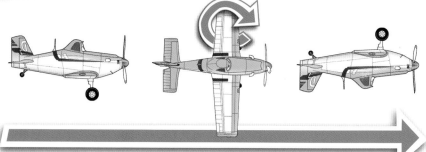

Barrel Roll

Ascend sharply while starting the roll, descending sharply after you peak and keep turning. Not for the faint hearted!

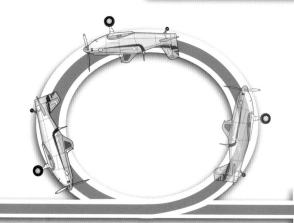

Inside Loop

Pick up speed, keep a steady nose and pull up hard, accelerating right through the loop. It is a neat trick; you have to perfect this one, kid!

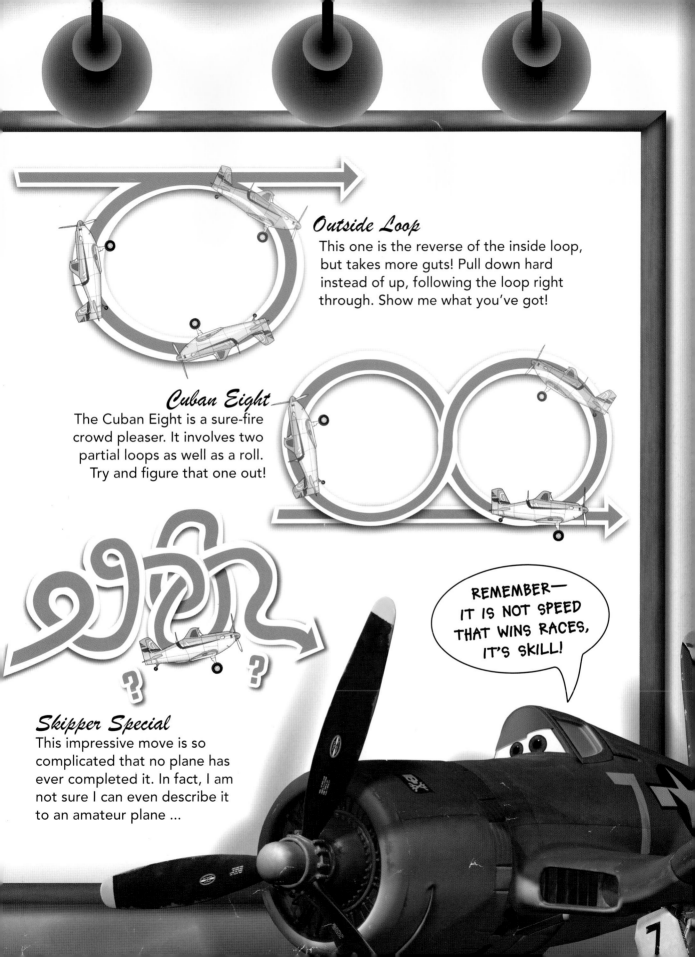

Outside Loop

This one is the reverse of the inside loop, but takes more guts! Pull down hard instead of up, following the loop right through. Show me what you've got!

Cuban Eight

The Cuban Eight is a sure-fire crowd pleaser. It involves two partial loops as well as a roll. Try and figure that one out!

REMEMBER— IT IS NOT SPEED THAT WINS RACES, IT'S SKILL!

Skipper Special

This impressive move is so complicated that no plane has ever completed it. In fact, I am not sure I can even describe it to an amateur plane ...

SPARKY

Kind and considerate Sparky is Skipper's faithful friend who uncomplainingly moves the old fighter plane around. The pragmatic tug from Propwash Junction has known Skipper for years, since they were both in the navy together. Sparky is a good-natured guy who quietly goes about his business, always willing to help others out!

TRICKY TASK

Spending most of your time with Skipper can be hard work. The grumpy war veteran can be difficult company. It is also not easy being the only one who knows why Skipper will not fly.

As residents of Propwash Junction, Sparky and Chug have known each other for years. They love to shoot the breeze and talk about exciting topics such as fuel flavors and cleaning cloths!

"GO TEAM DUSTERINO! YEAH!"

SPARKY'S TOP 3:
SKILLS AND TASKS

★ Transporting old planes around

★ Paint a stencil on bodywork

★ Set up a fantastic website

These forklifts do a lot of heavy lifting around Propwash Junction!

BRIGHT SPARK

Sparky is very modest, but there is not much that he cannot do. The enterprising tug can turn his forklifts to almost anything! He is also a mine of information and knows all the ins-and-outs of racing history.

Insignia of the Jolly Wrenches

RIGHT-HAND MAN

Skipper would not be able to function without Sparky. He transports him around, runs his errands, and keeps his secrets. Sparky is the most patient tug in Propwash Junction!

TRUE OR FALSE?

Sparky first met Skipper in Propwash Junction.

FALSE! They have known each other since their days in the navy.

Sparky wears the symbol of the US Navy

23

HOW TO QUALIFY

Only the very finest and fastest planes are allowed to compete in the Wings Around The Globe Rally. To sort out the first-rate racers from the winged wannabes, four qualifying time trials are held. These handy tips will help you navigate your way through the qualifiers.

1 BELIEVE IN YOURSELF

Some snooty planes have a very high opinion of themselves. Do not be put off by anybody who looks down their nose at a crop duster who wants to race. You can do this!

2 ENJOY THE ATTENTION

Do not be afraid of the crowds—listen to the cheers and lap up the atmosphere! If you enjoy yourself, you will perform better.

DO NOT GET STARSTRUCK

Some of the big-name racers automatically qualify for the race. Do not be overwhelmed by their presence—deep down they are just as nervous as you.

GIVE IT EVERYTHING

Focus your mind completely on the trial. Stay calm, but also feel fired up by the nerves in your engine. Now go out and give it your best shot—your friends are all rooting for you!

DID YOU KNOW?

Dusty qualifies for the WATG rally because another competitor is disqualified and Dusty takes his place.

DO NOT DESPAIR!

Very few make it through to the final rally, so do not feel down if you do not qualify. It is something to be proud of that you have made it this far!

WINGS AROUND THE GLOBE

The route for the Wings Around The Globe Rally goes right around the planet! The brave competitors fly for around 80 hours, over three continents, two oceans, and dozens of countries—and make only six stops!

ICELAND
2

GERMANY
3

1
NEW YORK

1 NEW YORK—ICELAND

DISTANCE
2,609 miles (4,199 km)

GEOGRAPHY
Open ocean with occasional icebergs

CHALLENGES
High winds and storms in the North Atlantic, sub-freezing temperatures

2 ICELAND—GERMANY

DISTANCE
1,477 miles (2,377 km)

GEOGRAPHY
Open ocean, land, forest

CHALLENGES
A Bavarian obstacle course—involves flying low but avoiding trees, all in the dark

3 GERMANY—INDIA

DISTANCE
4,077 miles (6,561 km)

GEOGRAPHY
Cities, countryside

CHALLENGES
Endurance—this is the second longest leg, demanding stamina and efficient use of fuel

DISTANCE
673 miles (1,084 km)

GEOGRAPHY
Mountains

CHALLENGES
Tricky mountain maneuvers through the Himalayas—dangerous peaks, forceful, freezing winds

INDIA—NEPAL
4

DISTANCE
2,075 miles (3,340 km)

GEOGRAPHY
Mountains, countryside

CHALLENGES
Poor visibility due to fog over mountains, staying focussed while fans give you a wave

DISTANCE
8,016 miles (12,901 km)

GEOGRAPHY
Open ocean

CHALLENGES
Endurance—this is the longest leg, and crosses the Pacific Ocean. Tropical storms possible

CHINA—MEXICO
6

NEPAL—CHINA
5

NEPAL
5

4

INDIA

6
CHINA

8
NEW YORK

7
MEXICO

7   **8**

MEXICO—NEW YORK—FINISH

DISTANCE
2,307 miles (3,712 km)

GEOGRAPHY
Desert, countryside, cities

CHALLENGES
Mental and physical strength, flying prowess, and sheer determination to go the final distance

THE COMPETITORS

As the bold racing rivals line up on the runway for the Wings Around The Globe Rally, the tension mounts. In the meantime, here are some facts about the main competitors. They may differ in size, design, and flying style, but they are all determined to win!

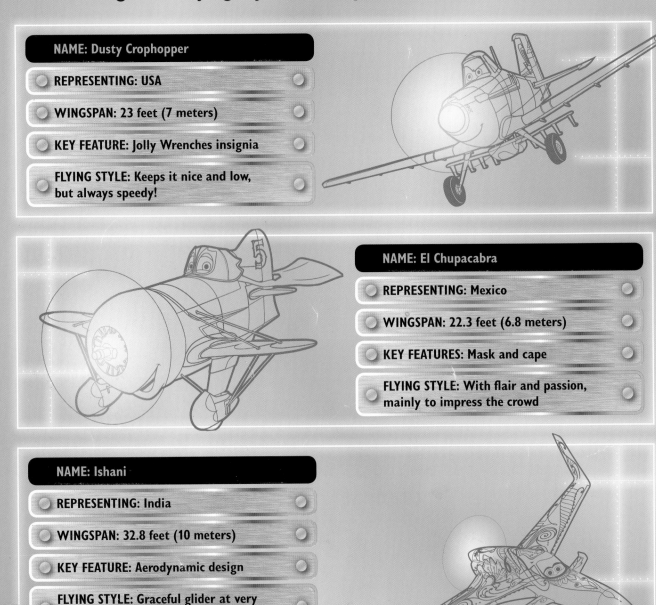

NAME: Dusty Crophopper

- REPRESENTING: USA
- WINGSPAN: 23 feet (7 meters)
- KEY FEATURE: Jolly Wrenches insignia
- FLYING STYLE: Keeps it nice and low, but always speedy!

NAME: El Chupacabra

- REPRESENTING: Mexico
- WINGSPAN: 22.3 feet (6.8 meters)
- KEY FEATURES: Mask and cape
- FLYING STYLE: With flair and passion, mainly to impress the crowd

NAME: Ishani

- REPRESENTING: India
- WINGSPAN: 32.8 feet (10 meters)
- KEY FEATURE: Aerodynamic design
- FLYING STYLE: Graceful glider at very high speeds

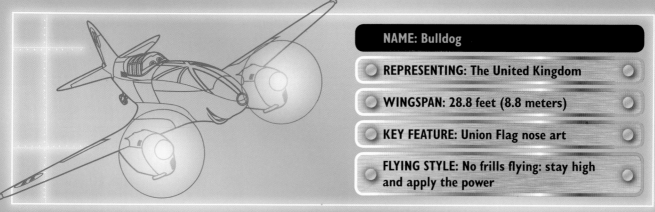

NAME: Bulldog

- REPRESENTING: The United Kingdom
- WINGSPAN: 28.8 feet (8.8 meters)
- KEY FEATURE: Union Flag nose art
- FLYING STYLE: No frills flying: stay high and apply the power

NAME: Ripslinger

- REPRESENTING: USA
- WINGSPAN: 26.2 feet (8 meters)
- KEY FEATURE: Light carbon-fiber frame
- FLYING STYLE: Takes the lead early, maintains pace from out in front

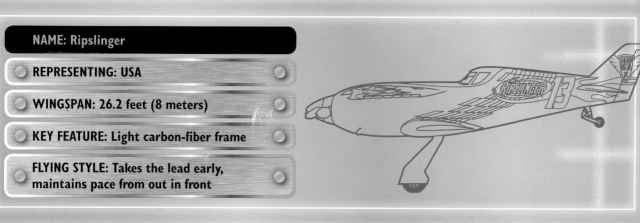

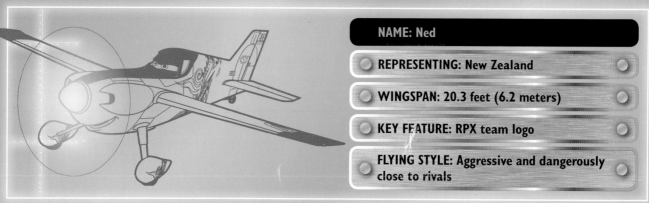

NAME: Ned

- REPRESENTING: New Zealand
- WINGSPAN: 20.3 feet (6.2 meters)
- KEY FEATURE: RPX team logo
- FLYING STYLE: Aggressive and dangerously close to rivals

NAME: Zed

- REPRESENTING: New Zealand
- WINGSPAN: 20.3 feet (6.2 meters)
- KEY FEATURE: RPX team logo
- FLYING STYLE: Whatever style his brother Ned happens to be doing!

RIPSLINGER

As three-time winner of the Wings Around The Globe Rally, racing legend Ripslinger is a rip-roaring success. Cool, arrogant, and very confident, Rip always goes for gold. But watch out! This high-flying champ does not always play fair and will do anything to win ...

TRUE OR FALSE?

Ripslinger has his own personal DJ and loves hip-hop.

TRUE! The DJ helps him to relax.

Streamlined tail using state-of-the-art design

The official Ripslinger logo

"YEAH! CAUGHT IN THE RIP-TIDE!"

ROTTEN RACER

Ripslinger has a sky-high opinion of himself and enjoys putting his rivals down. The arrogant airplane believes that only racing planes should race and that crop dusters should not even be allowed to compete!

NED AND ZED

Known as the Twin Turbos, Ned and Zed are not the sharpest planes on the runway. They spend most of their energy helping their boss Rip to win—usually by dastardly means!

Ripslinger is known throughout the racing world as the "Green Tornado." He finds that a little green smoke goes a long way!

Skyslycer Mark Five propeller, only used by Rip's racing team

FANTASTIC FANS

Ripslinger loves the attention of the crowd almost as much as he loves himself! There's nothing quite like hearing the roar of his adoring and loyal fans from all over the world.

BEHIND THE SCENES

It is every fan's dream to see what really happens backstage at the WATG Rally. In truth, it is always a bit chaotic in the competitor quarters! Busy tugs work on urgent repairs, racing legends rest in their hangars, and old racing friends catch up.

REFUEL AND RELAX

After a gruelling day racing, the competitors can be exhausted. Rest, relaxation, and sometimes repairs are required to regain strength for the next leg. The tugs work as quickly as they can to sort out any problems.

Most racers have personal mechanics for repairs

RESPECT AND RIVALRY

Behind the scenes most competitors get along very well and respect each other. Bulldog is not the friendliest, but he at least plays by the rules and is fair.

NEW KID ON THE BLOCK

To start with, Dusty does not know anybody and misses his friends back home. However, talking to them on the radio helps him with his homesickness.

Bulldog has one of the grandest hangars

After racing Dusty likes to stretch his wheels

DID YOU KNOW?

Ripslinger has his own personal DJ to play him music and often gets a buffer-massage in his hangar.

DUSTY'S DEN

Each racer has his own hangar and Dusty's is next to El Chu's. The bigger the star, the grander the hangar! Unsurprisingly, Dusty's is very plain.

EL CHUPACABRA

El Chupacabra, or simply El Chu to his amigos, is the Mexican indoor racing champion. His flamboyant and colorful character brings lots of passion, flair, and excitement to the sport. The larger than life racing plane always likes to be the center of attention!

El Chu races as number five

Green cape to swish about

SINGING STAR

El Chu loves to sing Mexican mariachi songs. The unlikely singing star has even released a CD of his favorite serenades called *Rudios de Motor* (meaning "engine noises")!

GOOD AMIGOS!

El Chu and Dusty are new to the WATG Rally and get on like a house on fire! El Chu gives Dusty new wings when his are damaged, proving what a good pal he is.

ROMANTIC RACER

If there is one thing that El Chu considers more important than racing, it is love. The romantic Mexican loves to woo the ladies with his cheesy chat-up lines and romantic acts. He easily falls helplessly nose-over-tail in love!

EL CHU'S TOP 3: ALTERNATIVE CAREERS

★ Mariachi recording artist

★ Daytime TV soap opera star

★ Leading romantic novelist

El Chu can be easily offended. When the British racer Bulldog pokes a little gentle fun at him, the melodramatic Mexican flounces off in a huff with a swish of his cape!

Mask to give a sense of mystery

Body is painted in the colors of the Mexican flag

TRUE OR FALSE?
El Chu gives Dusty a copy of his greatest hits CD as a present.

FALSE! He gives him two T33 wings when Dusty needs spare parts.

"THE HERO OF THE PEOPLE HAS ARRIVED!"

ON THE RACE TRACK

It is the moment that everyone has been waiting for—the official start of the Wings Around The Globe Rally from JFK International Airport in New York. This is by far the biggest, and most exciting, date in Dusty's racing career!

As the tension mounts, the starting flag is raised, ready to get the race started

WINGS AROUND THE GLOBE

PLANE PARADE

Led by last year's winner, Ripslinger, the racers emerge from the tunnel and taxi towards the runway. There is a deafening roar from the crowds as the excitement mounts!

A DREAM COME TRUE

Holy smokes! Dusty is overwhelmed by the occasion and finds it hard to believe it is actually happening. He has come such a long way in a short time!

FANTASTIC FANS

As confetti fills the air, noisy trucks and cars go nuts in the grandstand. They rev up their engines and shout for their favorite racer!

Excited fans are packed into the stands

DID YOU KNOW?

Ripslinger has won the last three WATG Rallies. Can he make it four?

CENTER OF ATTENTION

The planes face the crowds and the press knowing that they are also being watched by millions of TV viewers around the world. They are doing their best to not look too nervous!

WISH YOU WERE HERE

The Wings Around The Globe Rally takes Dusty to many different countries throughout Europe and Asia, as well as across two oceans. Although he loves his incredible adventure, Dusty also misses his friends in Propwash Junction. Time to send some postcards back home to let them know how he is getting along!

From Iceland

Hi Dottie,
Brrrrr! I am in Iceland and it is so cold, icicles have been forming on my sprayer! Today, as well as nearly getting killed by a ten-story iceberg, I am in last place. You were right all along—it WAS a crazy idea to enter this race. Miss you!
Your buddy, Dusty xxx

Dottie

Fill 'n' Fly Service

Station,

Propwash Junction,

Minnesota,

USA

Hey Chug,
I am in Germany! Not sure you would dig the music (it sounds like 100 tractors mooing), but you would love this crazy car I met called Franz. He actually has wings—and calls himself Von Fliegenhosen when he turns into a plane! It is a weird world out here.
Your friend, the Dustmeister!

Chug

Fill 'n' Fly Service

Station,

Propwash Junction,

Minnesota,

USA

Greetings from Germany!

Dear Leadbottom,
How are you coping
without me? Today I had
a tour of the amazing Taj
Mahal and flew over the
beautiful Indian countryside.
You would love it! There
are miles of fields here
that could be sprayed with
Vita-minamulch! Must fly,
bye for now! Dusty

Leadbottom
Propwash Junction,
Minnesota,
USA

HELLO FROM INDIA

A Nepalese Temple

Dear Skipper,
You are not going to believe
this, but I am in Nepal and I
am now first place! OK, I admit
that I did not completely follow
your advice and fly high over
the Himalayas (I actually flew
through a railway tunnel—
don't ask!), but I feel I could
even win this. Wish me luck!
                    Regards, Dusty

Skipper
Skipper's Hangar,
Propwash Junction,
Minnesota,
USA

Hi Sparky,
I've been flying over the Great
Wall of China. And it is great!
I am also still in first place and
have lots of fans cheering me
on. If I win, I think I may need
a website. Please could you
set one up for me when I get
home? That would be great!
Your friend, Dusty

Sparky
C/O Skipper's Hangar,
Propwash Junction,
Minnesota,
USA

The Great Wall of China

CHALLENGES OF THE RALLY

With so many dangers and difficulties along the way, the Wings Around The Globe Rally tests the endurance and abilities of the very strongest racers. Nerves of steel are required to even complete the race, let alone win!

TERRIFYING TERRAINS

Flying low through forests in Germany or maneuvering around snowy mountain ranges in the Himalayas means that there is a real chance of crashing.

DID YOU KNOW?

Even the most experienced racers can get into trouble. Bulldog almost crashes in Germany!

WILD WEATHER

Extreme weather can be expected in a round-the-world rally. From tropical storms in the Pacific to ice storms in Iceland, Dusty has to battle all kinds of weather challenges on his journey.

LOSING YOUR WAY

The route of the WATG Rally is so long that it is easy to go off-course. When Dusty loses his antenna he ends up lost at sea! Luckily, he bumps into navy jets Bravo and Echo just before he runs out of fuel.

FOUL PLAY

Ripslinger is determined to win, even if it means not playing fair. With the help of his rotten henchmen Ned and Zed, Rip steals Dusty's antenna so that he gets lost, and even forces Dusty to crash into the Pacific!

FALSE FRIENDSHIP

Sometimes it is simply hard to know who to trust. Dusty is double-crossed by Ishani when she advises him to fly low through the Himalayas. She misleads him in return for one of Ripslinger's special propellers.

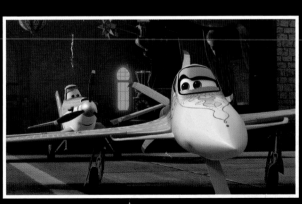

ISHANI

Indian racer Ishani is one of the most successful competitors around. The popular Pan-Asian champion is also the Mumbai Cup record holder. Her unique combination of grace, grit, and great skill has won her a huge following in her own country, as well as loyal admirers from all over the world.

With a rear propeller, sleek bodywork, and an extra pair of miniature wings known as canards, Ishani has a special aerodynamic advantage over her rivals!

Canard wings help with airspeed

TRUE OR FALSE?

Ishani was once named "Most Aerodynamic Racer" by a magazine.

TRUE! The magazine was Airsports Illustrated.

BEAUTY AND GRACE

With the elaborate patterns on her bodywork and her amazing aerodynamic design, Ishani is renowned in the racing world for her beauty. In fact, when Dusty first meets Ishani, he is completely lost for words!

SHIFTY ISHANI

At first it seems that Ishani could be a good friend to Dusty. But, her ambitious streak is so strong, she agrees to help Ripslinger ruin part of the race for Dusty—in return for a new propeller.

Winglets for greater flying efficiency

Beautiful patterns on her bodywork

MAKING AMENDS

Ishani is not all bad. To show Dusty how she is sorry for doing Ripslinger's dirty work, she gives him the Skyslycer Mark Five propeller, given to her by Ripslinger.

Extra-aerodynamic nose tip

ISHANI'S TOP 3:
THINGS TO SEE IN INDIA

⭐ **The Taj Mahal**

⭐ **The magnificent Himalayas**

⭐ **The beautiful countryside**

"I HAVE A BILLION FANS!"

OVERCOMING FEARS

The route of the Wings Around The Globe Rally is lined with dangers and terrifying tests of character. On many occasions Dusty has to dig deep and use all his determination to face his fears. However, the plucky plane from Propwash Junction soon proves he has the grit and the spirit to be a world-class racer!

TUNNEL TERROR

Dusty is on track for an easy route through the Himalayas following a railway line—until he meets a tunnel. He is very brave to enter the darkness, but even braver dodging the train on the way out!

DON'T LOOK DOWN

Of all the things that Dusty is scared of, his fear of heights is the most serious. To win the rally, Dusty knows that he must fly high into the clouds. It takes real guts for him to rise above his altitude anxiety!

DID YOU KNOW?

Skipper's nickname for somebody scared of heights is a "flat hatter," meaning a plane who flies too low!

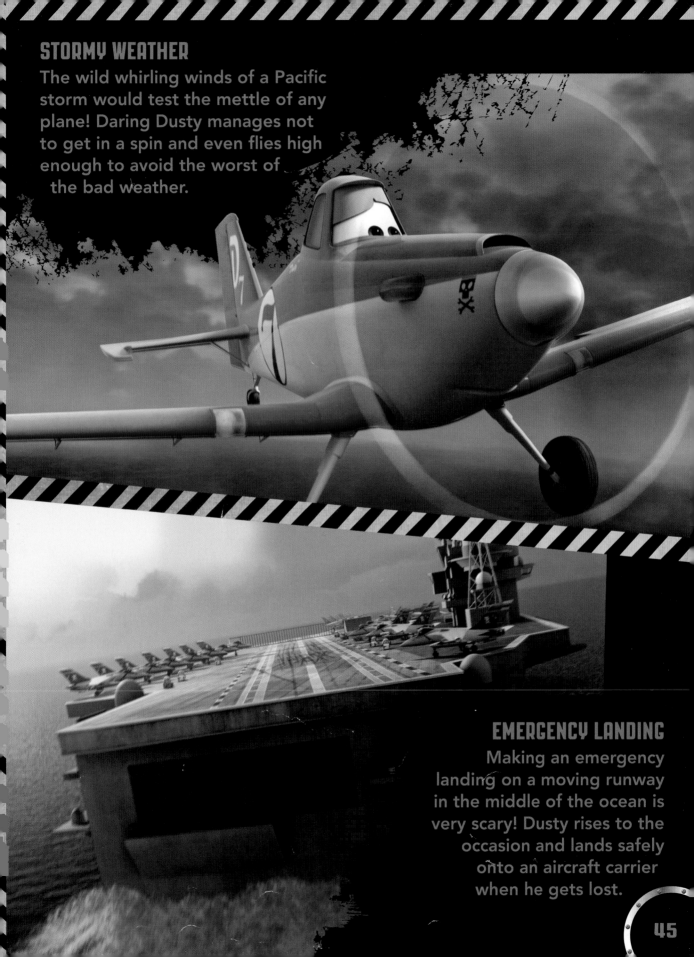

STORMY WEATHER

The wild whirling winds of a Pacific storm would test the mettle of any plane! Daring Dusty manages not to get in a spin and even flies high enough to avoid the worst of the bad weather.

EMERGENCY LANDING

Making an emergency landing on a moving runway in the middle of the ocean is very scary! Dusty rises to the occasion and lands safely onto an aircraft carrier when he gets lost.

BULLDOG

British racing veteran Bulldog has been around on the circuit for as long as anybody can remember. The champion of the European Cup air rally is a superior racer, with a tough approach to winning races! As far as the "Big Dog" is concerned, it's dog-eat-dog in the air!

TRUE OR FALSE?

Dusty calls Bulldog the Cockney Hound.

FALSE! He calls him the "Big Dog."

Patriotic Union Flag design

"THIS IS A COMPETITION! EVERY PLANE FOR HIMSELF!"

BULLDOG'S TOP 3:
TIPS FOR WINNING

★ Don't give away your racing secrets

★ Remember it's a competition!

★ Never show any emotion, lad

Extra powerful propellers

A BRITISH BULLDOG

Bulldog loves everything about Britain and is very patriotic. His tug even knows how to make him the perfect cup of British tea!

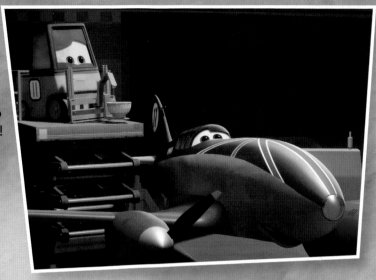

Bulldog races as number 11

When racing, Bulldog's years of experience are always an advantage in leading the pack. He is a master tactician with a knack for spectacular vertical turns.

GRATEFUL BRITON

Bulldog does not have much time for Dusty when they first meet. However, he soon loses his stiff upper lip when Dusty helps save him from crashing in Germany!

BULLDOG'S BARK

On first meeting, Bulldog can come across as unfriendly, making fun of his competitors. But his bark is definitely worse than his bite! In fact, Bulldog is a good sport who has lots of respect for his fellow racers.

Paintwork is the colors of the Union Flag of the United Kingdom

THE LOWDOWN ON DUSTY

Dusty and his incredible success have left a strong impression on everyone who knows him. In fact, it is impossible not to have an opinion about Dusty! So what do the people who know him really think?

"Dusty? His canopy has always been full o' fertilizer. He'd best forget this air racin' nonsense and get back to crop dustin'! I can't spray these fields all by myself."

– Leadbottom, Dusty's boss

"When I met Dusty, he was impulsive, stubborn, and just plain sloppy ... but he's the most instinctive flyer I have ever taught. Plus he has the fighting spirit of the Jolly Wrenches."

– Skipper, Dusty's instructor

"Dusty is my brother from another manufacturer! Everyone in Propwash Junction is real proud of him. Especially me! Hey, do you wanna buy a Dusty antenna ball? Commemorative whistle? Oil mug?"

– Chug, Dusty's best friend

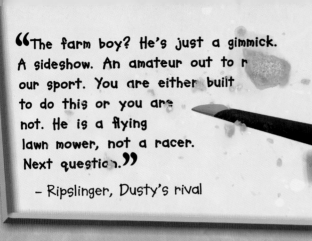

"The farm boy? He's just a gimmick. A sideshow. An amateur out to r[uin] our sport. You are either built to do this or you are not. He is a flying lawn mower, not a racer. Next question."

— Ripslinger, Dusty's rival

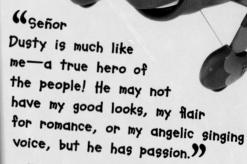

"Crophopper is a breath of fresh air for air racing. He was built to dust crops, but now he is dusting the competition! We will be seeing a lot of him in the years to come— his career is just taking off."

— Brent Mustangburger,
Racing Sports Network anchorman

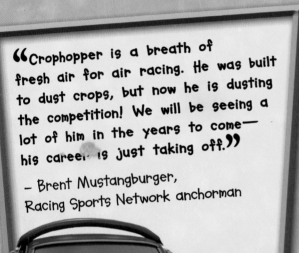

"Señor Dusty is much like me—a true hero of the people! He may not have my good looks, my flair for romance, or my angelic singing voice, but he has passion."

— El Chupacabra, WATG competitor

"Dusty is an inspiration to all us little planes in the world! He is living proof that you should never judge a plane by its wings. Or a car by its wheels, for that matter."

— Franz / Von Fliegenhosen,
flying car and Dusty's
biggest fan

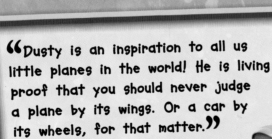

U.S.S. DWIGHT D. FLYSENHOWER

US Navy aircraft carrier U.S.S. *Dwight D. Flysenhower* is home to the Jolly Wrenches, a courageous squadron of fighter planes. The crew's combination of naval know-how and flying flair is unrivalled!

STRONG LEADER

Dwight D. Flysenhower is firmly in control of all his crew. From the moment of leaving port, this stern-looking boat lets everyone on board know he is the boss. His orders are always obeyed!

The admiral always has a watchful eye on the comings and goings on deck

All the fighter jets wear the Jolly Wrenches insignia

Support crew are always on hand to help

THE CATAPULT

U.S.S. *Flysenhower* has all the latest hi-tech equipment, such as the catapult. This device propels planes to a speed of 160 knots in 2 seconds!

TEAM U.S.S. *FLYSENHOWER*

The fighter jets might get all the attention, but they would not get far without their talented support crew. The committed tugs on board are just as vital as the other Jolly Wrenches.

DID YOU KNOW?

The ship has a "Wall of Fame," listing every single mission undertaken by the Jolly Wrenches.

Dusty gets to visit U.S.S. *Dwight D. Flysenhower* when he is rescued by two of the aircraft carrier's jet planes. On board, Dusty learns that his mentor Skipper only ever completed one mission. Skipper reveals over the radio that he lost his squadron on this mission, and vowed never to fly again.

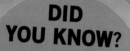

BRAVO AND ECHO

Brave US Navy planes Bravo and Echo have nerves of steel. Always cool in a crisis and on a mission to make the world a safer place, these guys protect the skies! Bravo and Echo are stationed on board the U.S.S. *Dwight D. Flysenhower*, and are part of the Jolly Wrenches, a group of jets with a long history.

Twin tails to help with smooth maneuvers

Missiles to keep enemies at bay

"GO WIN IT FOR THE WRENCHES, DUSTY!"

BRAVO

Bravo has a sharp mind and an outstanding military record. Years of training has meant he is one of the navy's top troops. His military style of talking, tough exterior, and weapons display can scare off any enemy.

The aircraft carrier U.S.S. *Dwight D. Flysenhower* is one of the largest vessels around. It is on a mission to keep the Pacific Ocean safe!

NAVY PLANES' TOP 3: MILITARY TERMS

★ "Bogey" = unidentified aircraft

★ "Bingo field" = landing spot

★ "Call the ball" = asking a plane which of the landing lights he can see

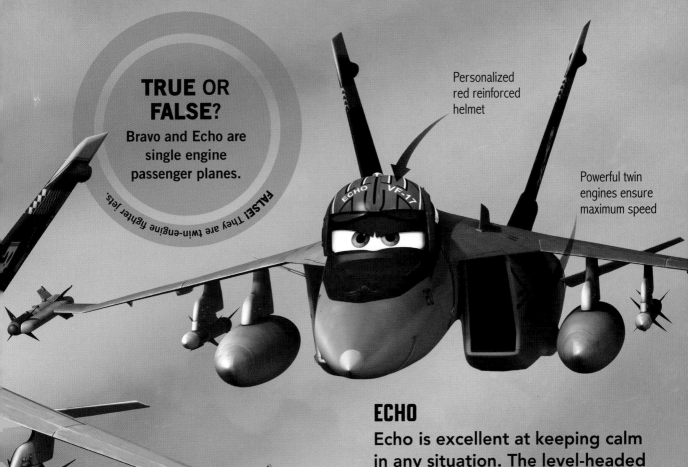

TRUE OR FALSE?

Bravo and Echo are single engine passenger planes.

FALSE! They are twin-engine fighter jets.

Personalized red reinforced helmet

Powerful twin engines ensure maximum speed

ECHO

Echo is excellent at keeping calm in any situation. The level-headed Super Hornet always appears in control, which helps to put those around him at ease. Echo can be relied upon in any tricky situation!

PACIFIC PATROL

Dusty may feel foolish for running out of fuel, but he is very glad to be met by Bravo and Echo. The helpful heroes guide him back to the safety of their ship.

Bravo and Echo are huge racing fans. After helping Dusty refuel, they urge him to go on and win the Wings Around The Globe Rally. After all, Dusty bears the Jolly Wrenches insignia of their squadron! To victory!

WHAT KIND OF RACER ARE YOU?

Do you want to win the Wings Around The Globe Rally? Have you got what it takes to compete against the elite? Before you consider making your move, take our quick personality test to work out what sort of racer you are. This could help you plan for success, or deal with failure!

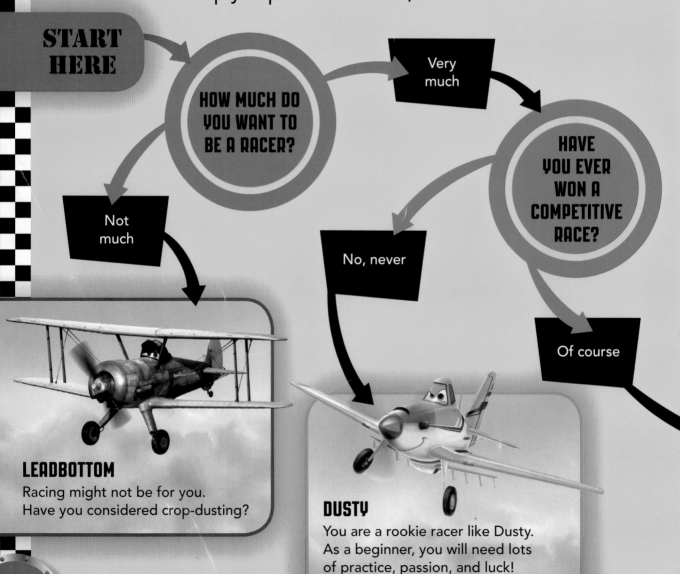

START HERE

HOW MUCH DO YOU WANT TO BE A RACER?

Very much

Not much

HAVE YOU EVER WON A COMPETITIVE RACE?

No, never

Of course

LEADBOTTOM
Racing might not be for you. Have you considered crop-dusting?

DUSTY
You are a rookie racer like Dusty. As a beginner, you will need lots of practice, passion, and luck!

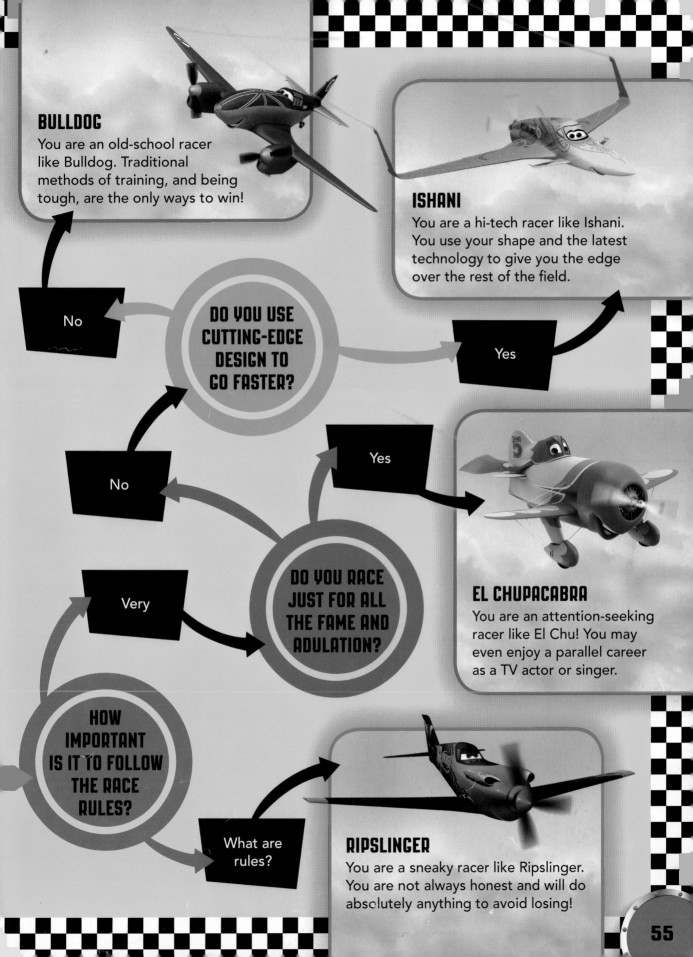

BULLDOG

You are an old-school racer like Bulldog. Traditional methods of training, and being tough, are the only ways to win!

ISHANI

You are a hi-tech racer like Ishani. You use your shape and the latest technology to give you the edge over the rest of the field.

No

DO YOU USE CUTTING-EDGE DESIGN TO GO FASTER?

Yes

No

Yes

EL CHUPACABRA

You are an attention-seeking racer like El Chu! You may even enjoy a parallel career as a TV actor or singer.

Very

DO YOU RACE JUST FOR ALL THE FAME AND ADULATION?

HOW IMPORTANT IS IT TO FOLLOW THE RACE RULES?

What are rules?

RIPSLINGER

You are a sneaky racer like Ripslinger. You are not always honest and will do absolutely anything to avoid losing!

A HELPING HAND

It is said that all successful racers need a good team behind them, and Dusty is no exception. In fact, without the help of his friends, Dusty would still be spraying crops around Propwash Junction. Not only have Dusty's friends been there at the right time to lend a hand, but they have also given him the confidence and courage to carry on.

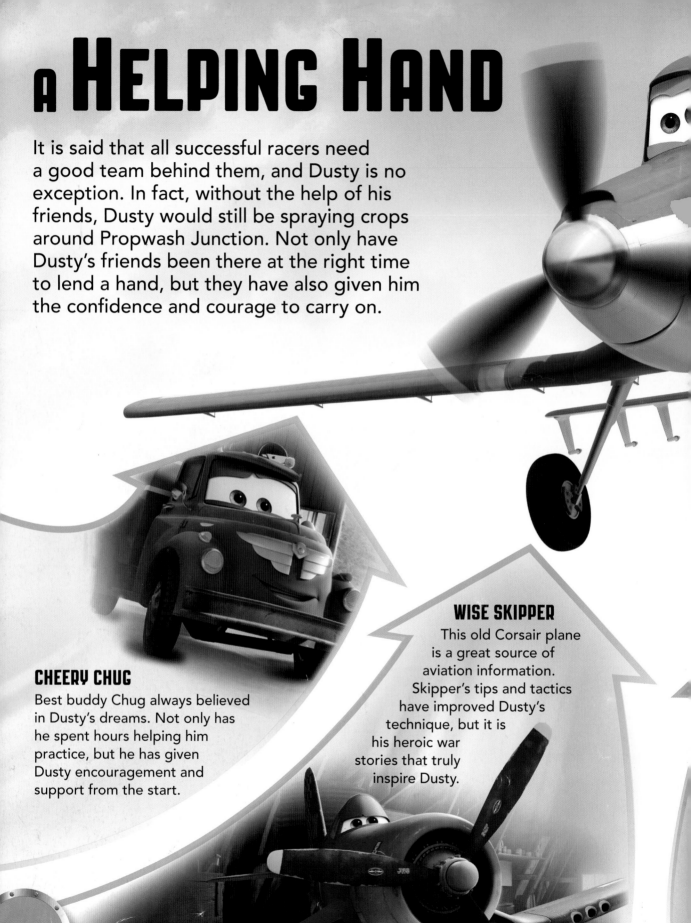

CHEERY CHUG

Best buddy Chug always believed in Dusty's dreams. Not only has he spent hours helping him practice, but he has given Dusty encouragement and support from the start.

WISE SKIPPER

This old Corsair plane is a great source of aviation information. Skipper's tips and tactics have improved Dusty's technique, but it is his heroic war stories that truly inspire Dusty.

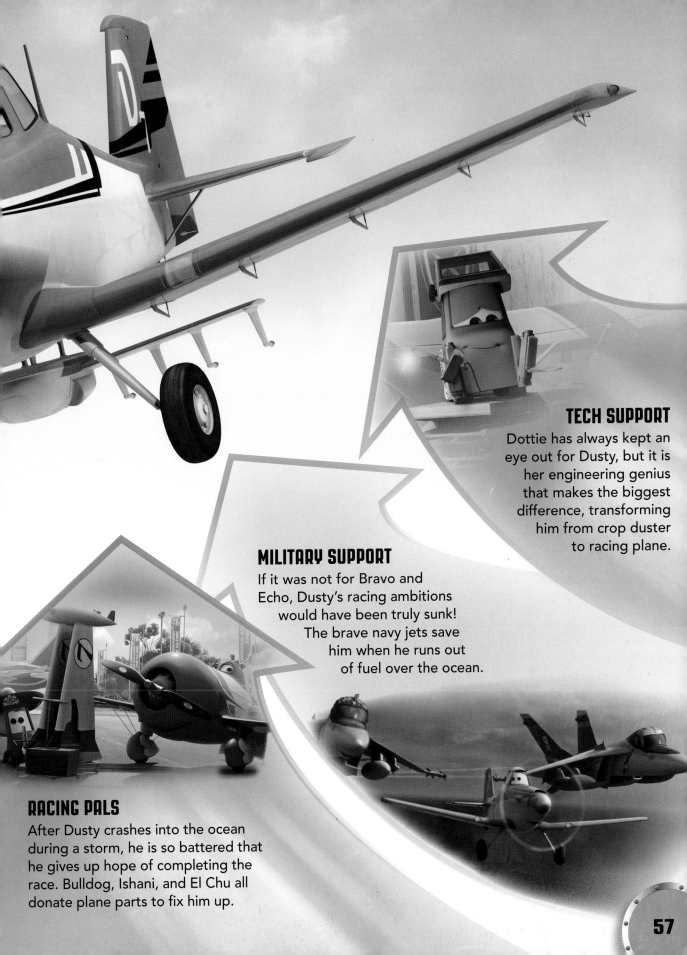

TECH SUPPORT

Dottie has always kept an eye out for Dusty, but it is her engineering genius that makes the biggest difference, transforming him from crop duster to racing plane.

MILITARY SUPPORT

If it was not for Bravo and Echo, Dusty's racing ambitions would have been truly sunk! The brave navy jets save him when he runs out of fuel over the ocean.

RACING PALS

After Dusty crashes into the ocean during a storm, he is so battered that he gives up hope of completing the race. Bulldog, Ishani, and El Chu all donate plane parts to fix him up.

DUSTY THE SUPERSTAR!

Dusty's unexpected success propels him to overnight stardom. Everybody loves the story of how a small-town crop duster came from nowhere to win the Wings Around The Globe Rally! Dusty is now a regular on the Racing Sports Network (RSN), the number one sports TV station worldwide.

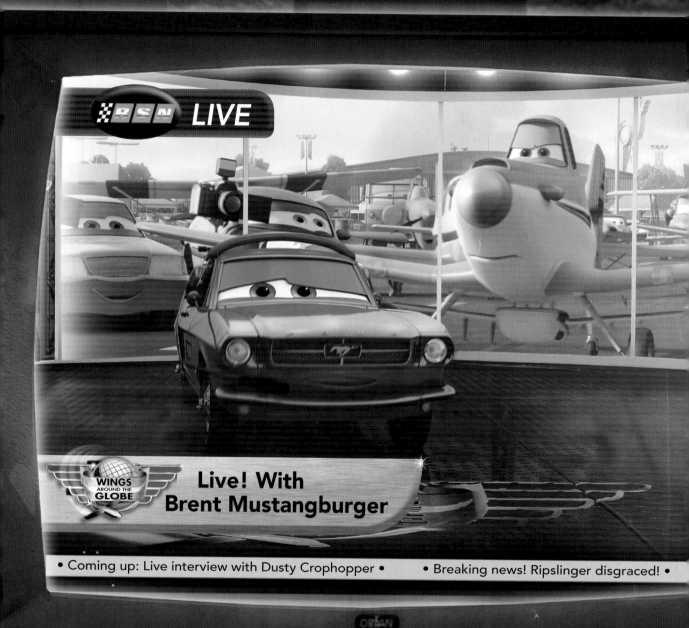

RSN LIVE

WINGS AROUND THE GLOBE

Live! With
Brent Mustangburger

• Coming up: Live interview with Dusty Crophopper •   • Breaking news! Ripslinger disgraced! •

Racing's Newest Star

Being famous has its drawbacks. Dusty must get used to reporters from TV and newspapers thrusting microphones under his nose wherever he goes.

Dusty's pals back in Propwash Junction follow all the action on the Racing Sports Network. Despite their friend now being world famous, they know that it has not changed him. The cool-headed crop duster might be a champion, but he is still their old buddy Dusty!

Brent Mustangburger is the best known anchor on RSN. The legendary presenter is even more famous than many of the racers! His insight and enthusiasm makes for some entertaining commentary.

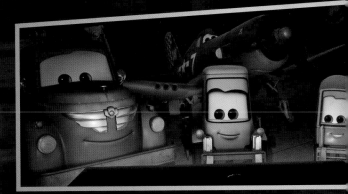

Racing fans all around the world love Dusty. From cars and tugs in a London pub to planes in a Japanese sushi bar, everybody is rooting for the underdog to win. When Dusty actually does win, they all go crazy with delight! Go Dusty!

We Have a Winner!

Q&A

The latest racing sensation answers YOUR questions!

Breezy McSwoopson
Racing Plane Weekly Staff Writer

He is the crop duster from Propwash Junction that has gone from farm to fame in a matter of weeks by winning the prestigious Wings Around The Globe Rally! Dusty Crophopper reveals the secrets behind his success.

Photo: Lisa Robb

"Always believe in yourself!"

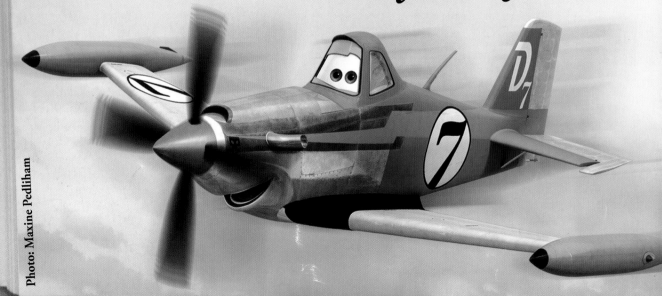

Photo: Maxine Pedliham

Question *What do your Propwash Junction pals think of you?*

Answer

Photo: Laura Gilbert

My buddies back home are even more excited about winning than I am! Chug, Dottie, Sparky, and especially Skipper are all very proud of me. But nothing else has changed—I am still their pal Dusty, the crop duster from Minnesota.

What did you enjoy most about the race? **Question**

Answer

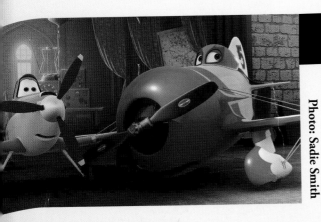

Photo: Sadie Smith

It was amazing to be able to travel the world and see new places! I loved making lots of new friends, too. El Chu from Mexico was my best buddy among the racers. He has already invited me to appear on his new album of modern Mexican songs!

Question *What was the most valuable lesson you learned?*

Answer

Photo: Rhys Thomas

To not be intimidated and always believe in myself. Ripslinger told me I could never win, but I went on to beat him! I proved to myself that I was strong enough to compete with the best—and I feel proud of myself.

FROM CROP DUSTER TO RACING PLANE

Dusty has been on an amazing journey in more ways than one. Not only has he traveled the world, but he has also turned into a real racer, learning to think like a winner on the way. He has also had to undergo physical changes at different stages of the race, transforming him from crop duster to racing champion!

PROUD MOMENT

As Dusty practices with Skipper for the rally he gets better and better. A stencil of the Jolly Wrenches insignia, Skipper's old squadron, is painted on his nose. This helps him feel like a true racing ace.

WORN OUT!

As an agricultural plane, Dusty's engine simply cannot cope with going at full power for long periods of time. Even when just practicing, bits of Dusty start to wear out! How will he ever cope with a real race?

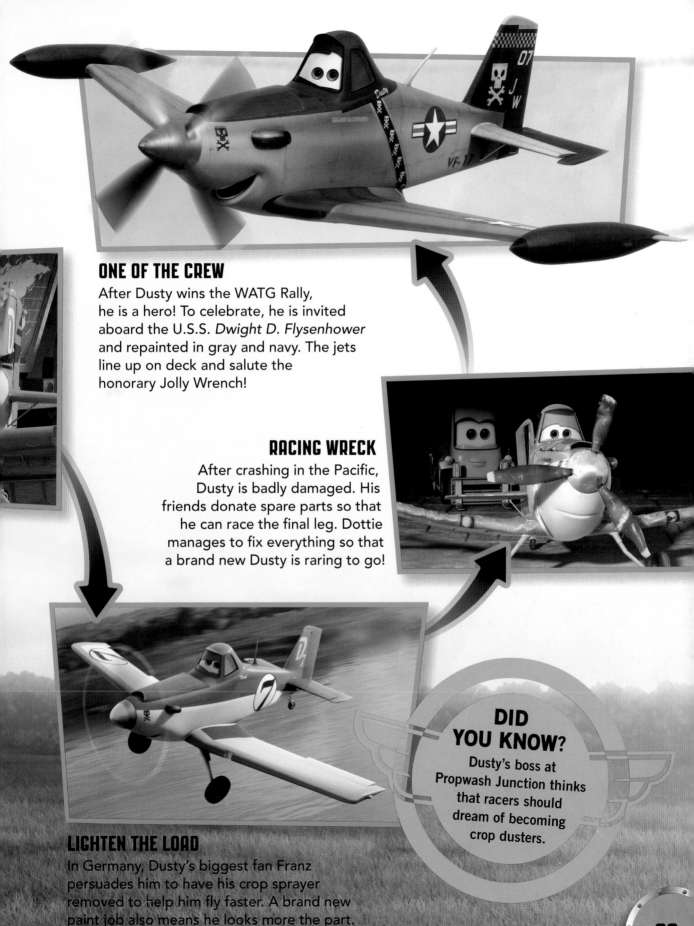

ONE OF THE CREW

After Dusty wins the WATG Rally, he is a hero! To celebrate, he is invited aboard the U.S.S. *Dwight D. Flysenhower* and repainted in gray and navy. The jets line up on deck and salute the honorary Jolly Wrench!

RACING WRECK

After crashing in the Pacific, Dusty is badly damaged. His friends donate spare parts so that he can race the final leg. Dottie manages to fix everything so that a brand new Dusty is raring to go!

LICHTEN THE LOAD

In Germany, Dusty's biggest fan Franz persuades him to have his crop sprayer removed to help him fly faster. A brand new paint job also means he looks more the part.

DID YOU KNOW?

Dusty's boss at Propwash Junction thinks that racers should dream of becoming crop dusters.

ACKNOWLEDGMENTS

LONDON, NEW YORK,
MELBOURNE, MUNICH, AND DELHI

Senior Editors Sadie Smith, Elizabeth Dowsett
Senior Designers Lisa Robb, Lynne Moulding
Design by Lisa Robb and Rhys Thomas
Pre-Production Producer Marc Staples
Senior Producer Danielle Smith
Managing Editor Laura Gilbert
Design Manager Maxine Pedliham
Art Director Ron Stobbart
Publishing Manager Julie Ferris
Publishing Director Simon Beecroft

First Published in the United States in 2013
by DK Publishing, 345 Hudson Street,
New York, New York 10014

10 9 8 7 6 5 4 3 2 1
001–188340–July/13

Copyright © 2013 Disney Enterprises, Inc.
All rights reserved

Mustang™ is a trademark of Ford Motor Company

Page design copyright © 2013 Dorling Kindersley Limited

All rights reserved under International and Pan-American Copyright
Conventions. No part of this publication may be reproduced,
stored in a retrieval system, or transmitted in any form or by any means,
electronic, mechanical, photocopying, recording, or otherwise,
without the prior written permission of the copyright owner.

Published in Great Britain by Dorling Kindersley Limited

DK books are available at special discounts when purchased in bulk
for sales promotions, premiums, fund-raising, or educational use.
For details, contact: DK Publishing Special Markets,
345 Hudson Street, New York, New York 10014
Special Sales@dk.com

A CIP catalog record for this book
is available from the Library of Congress

ISBN 978-1-4654-0268-4

Color reproduction by Alta Image, UK
Printed and bound in the US by Lake Book Manufacturing, Inc.

DK would like to thank Laura Nickoll for proofreading, Chelsea Alon,
Caroline Egan, Ryan Ferguson, Tony Fejeran, and Heather Knowles
at Disney Publishing, and Jeff Howard, Paul Gerard, David Siegel,
and Tony DeSimone at Disney Toon Studios.

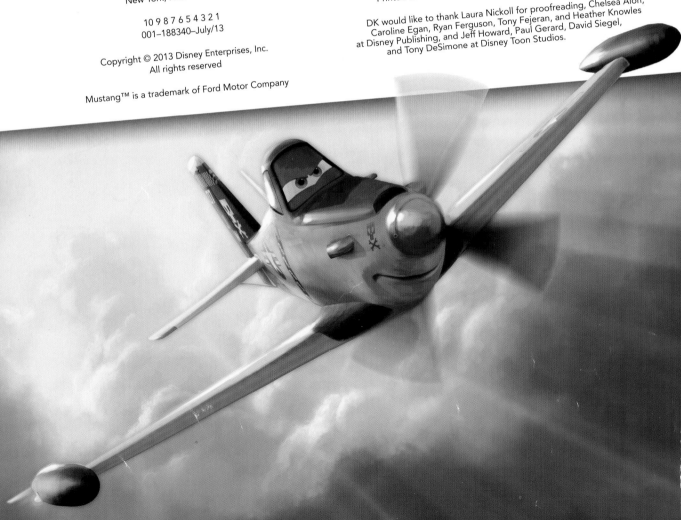